Joni Mitchell F
Life

Liverpool 1974 - 1985

Chris Grayling

Dedication

This is for anyone further down my family tree than me

© 2022 Chris Grayling

Also by Chris Grayling and available on Amazon:

The Neil Mackenzie trilogy

The Big Keep

The Big Sister

The Big Finish

More Neil Mackenzie

A Week is a Long Time

Death on a Cruise

Schooldays Autobiography

Diana Rigg Ruined My Life

Preface

Clearly Ms Mitchell didn't ruin my life – rather her magical songs enhanced my own and my friends' lives while we were at university. In many ways her lyrics were the background commentary on the apparent elusiveness of love. A better title for this would have been something like *Joni Mitchell – The Soundtrack of My Youth*, but the one I chose provided a neater link to the previous story of my boyhood.

And an apology – one or two stories below are merely repeats from *Diana Rigg Ruined My Life* because I clearly wasn't sure when they happened – which sort of proves what is probably self-evident anyway – that as we grow older our stories become less and less reliable!

Introduction

If you have already read *Diana Rigg Ruined My Life*, the first instalment of my autobiography, you will know that it finished as my schooldays ended in June 1974. At the time of publication I was sixty-two and had absolutely no intention of trying to write any more about my early life: mainly because, as far as I was concerned, it was better forgotten. You will also remember that my main motivation for writing down some of my garbled memories was for the benefit of my daughters - so that there is a written record rather than, in the near future, no one or only a dribbling old man to ask about the past. All of us die, taking our memories with us.

Unlike a Neil Mackenzie novel where I can throw in a few witty lines or a hot sex scene, real life is much more prosaic. If I seemed like an unhappy teenager back then I deduced that my university days would also come across as ones of unrelenting misery: hardly the kind of material that makes for a gripping narrative. However, when I actually came to examine those years more forensically, I found that I actually had a lot of fun. Yes, from the perspective of middle age they seemed to have the flavour of an introspective song from a Joni Mitchell album, but that proved to be only a superficial impression. Maybe it's the same for most older people – when they look back on their youthful selves one of the first phrases that spring to mind is

'WTF' because by then they've realised how lucky they were to be young, single and arthritis-free. It's a well-worn cliché but youth really is wasted on the young. Without exception, all of them need a wise adult in their lives to advise them on how to enjoy themselves while they can.

Young people generally live their lives under two misapprehensions – firstly, that despite all the evidence to the contrary they will live forever and, secondly, that they are special, even if that delusion doesn't include the belief that they are marked out by fate for an assignment that might possibly influence world history. The reality is that you *will* die and, once you are dead, hardly anybody will remember you after (if you have any) your children or possibly your grandchildren have gone.

When death seems as if it lies decades into the future we tend to equate our own mortality with a kind of theoretical immortality. I lived my early years, for example, as if I would live forever (on several occasions in youth I calculated that I would be 45 in the year 2000 and simultaneously thinking that 45 wasn't even old and was an age away) and was also relaxed about my own intrinsic specialness, even if the reality of my existence screamed 'loser'.

When Rog, one of my closest and longest lasting friends read this he told me that we had discussed this several times, one of which was on our nightly cycle ride home from school. Apparently

Bill Bush, my other great childhood friend, said that there was no point in worrying because most people were dead by 45 anyway. But Bill always was a glass half-empty type.

Besides, my time in Liverpool occurred around forty years ago, so actually remembering what happened is almost impossible. Yes, I didn't keep a diary (now I think that we should all use one, however disorganised, because the alternative guarantees memories will be lost or distorted) which would have made everything simpler. Mind you, I've always been pretty sure that, back then, I was an even bigger dick than I am now so perhaps there's the opposing argument regarding keeping a diary.

Because I've always been convinced of my own youthful idiocy, I've never given a lot of thinking time to past memories. For reasons which will become apparent, a regular tendency to be crass and immature usually negated any good behaviour on my part. I'm afraid the die was cast with my first girlfriend Ginny (not her real name) in *Diana Rigg Ruined My Life*. At university I continued to be unlucky in love and seemed to derive some masochistic pleasure in being regularly unhappy. Christ, I was a jerk.

And then something happened to make me reconsider writing about those days: I was having dinner this summer, four years after publishing *Diana Rigg...*, with some English friends. Among them was a couple from Liverpool. Jean - the wife - obviously, (here's an interesting fact - most women in Liverpool are actually called Jean) went to Liverpool Girls' College, which I immediately thought was the school in which I did my teacher training back in January or February 1980. She was there then so I might have taught her! Cue lots of excited reminiscing - up until that moment I hadn't given my teacher training weeks in Liverpool a second thought in over 40 years. In those days I lived on the legendary Hope St in the university's Philharmonic Court halls of residence and LGC fitted all the criteria that I could remember - similar building and location and an all-girls school. Theresa, my wife, says that I let it slip that I thought all the girls at LGC were as thick as shit, but this didn't seem to faze Jean. Theresa is probably lying anyway.

Something as mundane as to the identity of my teacher training school sparked renewed interest in my university days – if I was hazy on those details then it began to bother me that everything else was also disappearing into the abyss of time. All I could remember about my teacher training was a pleasant fellow who mentored me for my short time at LGC. I couldn't remember his name but it slowly dawned on me that he was some kind of amateur magician. In fact one of the only things I can remember from my many classroom observations was watching him do the old chalk-in-the-ear-and-out-of-the-mouth trick in front of some year eight girls. I must have been impressed because I used it with every class I ever taught for the next 30 years. His name, however, wouldn't come back to me.

So, with Jean's prompting, I did a bit of digging and contacted an English teacher of the era from LGC who, frustratingly, couldn't remember the wannabe Harry Potter of the maths teaching world either. This should have set alarm bells ringing but I ploughed on convinced of the veracity of my memory.

Everywhere else, however, drew me a blank until one night a few weeks later I was perusing a map of Hope St and the surrounding area and I saw a road called Blackburne Place. And then I remembered – the school I did my teacher training at wasn't LGC; it was actually Liverpool Institute High School for Girls or Blackburne Place School. And I wasn't there in January or February 1980 but in 1981, by which time LGC had closed anyway. The next day a former pupil of Blackburne House told me on Facebook that my mentor was called Peter Rupert Everett who was still alive in 2018 and *did* like magic.

The net result of finding out Mr Everett's name is my decision to write about my eleven years in Liverpool. I needed to put the record in my mind straight – literally – and even if my own life isn't that compelling, those times in that city were. I'd like to say that the book is as much a story of the city and its people as it is of my often cringeworthy existence, but it's mostly about me. Nevertheless, I hope you enjoy it anyway.

1: My First Term, October – December 1974

I don't remember much about the weeks leading up to my leaving home. It's all lost in the sands of time. I think I must have been both apprehensive at leaving the comfort of home and excited at the prospect of seeing Ginny and going to university. Of course I took everything for granted: it's what young people do. I knew that I had to leave home but it wasn't the academic challenges that made me nervous. It was rather more to do with how I would miss my friends and mum and the comforts of the flat. And, if I'm honest, Ginny loomed larger on my horizons than mathematics.

Back then, so far as university education was concerned, the government were much more enlightened than they are today. For example, I didn't have to worry about paying back a student loan. I would be in receipt of a grant that was supposed to see me through until the following June and, as my mum didn't have any money, I was guaranteed the maximum amount on offer. During the summers I could also sign on at the labour exchange in Teignmouth even if I was secretly working at Terry Crump's hotel.

I managed to get everything into a huge cheap blue suitcase which I hauled down to Dawlish station one Sunday in early October where I got on a train to join John Phillips and Bob Offord who were both going to Liverpool as well. I knew John from my class at school, a likeable gregarious type. He was tall with long curly brown hair parted in the middle and had a cheerful, optimistic character. On the other hand I'd never met Bob before because he came from the year above me. Still, he seemed like a pleasant and friendly enough sort and the trip to Liverpool Lime Street station passed agreeably.

As the train advanced northwards, the stations at Birmingham, Crewe and Runcorn looked more and more alien to us. The North seemed, and is, completely different to Devon – it was dirtier, there were more towns, houses and people and it had factories instead of farms and fields. I'd only ever seen industry and rows of terraced houses on the telly. We were inwardly spellbound and apprehensive while outwardly taking it in our stride as you might expect three cocky teenagers to do.

As the journey progressed and we approached the outskirts of the city through what seemed like miles of railway cuttings, I think we all realised we were at the beginning of a new and exciting chapter in our lives: Liverpool was as different to South Devon as it was possible to imagine. I can't vouch for John and Bob, but I for one had never knowingly had a conversation with a northerner before, let alone a scouser, and I was as green as the greenest grass on an Irish lawn.

At Lime Street Station we hauled our huge bags off the train and all three of us squeezed into a taxi up to the Carnatic Halls of residence near leafy Sefton Park, three or so miles from the city centre. Here I parted company with John and Bob because they had been allocated different halls of residence on the other side of the Carnatic site. I was in Morton House which, as I approached it with my huge suitcase in tow, looked modern and soulless. I think it was a dry, chilly autumn day and much colder than the milder climes of Devon. There were yellow and russet-coloured leafed trees scattered around and my new home only looked a few years old at the most. I can't remember how I was registered but I ended up in a room on the third and top floor of B Block.

I had a single bed, bedside cabinet, wardrobe, a table and chair and a view of a leafy car park where parents were bravely depositing their offspring. On my corridor there appeared to be twelve or so rooms plus a small kitchen, some toilets and showers as well as a room with an ironing board and a washing machine. I ran into a couple of students and we exchanged pleasantries before I escaped back into the security of my digs. There were no mobile phones back then so all I had was a newly bought radio from my mum to keep me company.

The student in the room next to mine was a guy called Rupert Morgan. It's funny that I remember his name because we were never friends. He was the first public schoolboy I think I'd ever met. He was tall and bespectacled, spoke in a posh accent and came across as entitled as fuck. I sensed the bravado was a smoke screen and ignored all the flannel. Maybe he and I and some others all went over to Carnatic Hall at teatime to eat but I simply don't know.

The only other thing that sticks in my mind from that day was going out in the evening with John and Bob to a pub down in Allerton. God knows who we went with or what we talked about - all I can remember is ordering some drinks and thinking the barman was taking the piss when he asked me if I wanted a pint of Tetley's. Up until that point I'd only ever heard of Tetley's Tea.

So what about my first few days at university? Well, if I'm honest I don't remember an awful lot about them either. I ate breakfast and dinner in Carnatic Hall, at the time a modern, well-appointed school canteen where we filed in to be served food of a dubious standard which we then ate in a large dining hall on the first floor. I usually went into breakfast alone at eight before the rush but accompanied anyone else who was going from B Block for dinner at six-ish. Downstairs in Carnatic Hall was the bar which was surprisingly comfortable and had the air of a hotel lounge.

My days were spent at the university where I attended lectures, sat in a library somewhere trying to study or just walked around aimlessly. Tuesday afternoons were the worst when I was timetabled to do a three hour physics practical. It was painfully boring because I didn't have the necessary level of competence in electrical circuitry needed to derive any benefit from the course and none of the staff seemed willing to give me much of a guiding hand. If I'd been more proactive I'm sure I could have made more of a success of those afternoons but my heart wasn't in it.

As you'll soon see, Ginny departed from my life in a matter of weeks. After that the overriding emotion that engulfed me was one of loneliness. The feeling would pass after several months, and in a year or two I came to think of Liverpool as home rather than Dawlish. But for those few weeks the memory of the flat and mum and my familiar routine left a gaping gap in my soul.

In the early days I caught a bus from the site down to the university. It occurs to me that it was on a return ride back from the campus one day that another student confirmed to me that I was depressed. He or she revealed that waking up after six hours sleep meant that the person concerned was mentally down. It was a Eureka moment – I had been waking up very early and I realised that this was collaborating evidence of my own suspicions regarding my state of mind. Of course, now I'm in my sixties and visit the bathroom at least twice a night I would happily accept the luxury of six hours uninterrupted slumber in a heartbeat. Back then, however, I remember being miffed when I stirred at around 6 am. It's another reality of middle-age – sleeping through the night is only possible if drug-induced - something the young are blissfully unaware of.

The University's campus felt new and unfamiliar. It was a combination of modern architecture built next to more traditional buildings, all of which housed various departments. Someone told me that our students' union building was one of the largest in Europe and that at 7000 our student numbers dwarfed most other institutions (these days of course, student numbers everywhere have multiplied, so that 7000 is now a very small deal indeed). The Union building was conveniently opposite the Maths and Oceanography building which seemed like a funny marriage of academic disciplines to me. Still, I knew fuck all about the workings of university departments so who was I to question anything?

For the first week, called 'Freshers' Week', there weren't any lectures so, after visiting the maths department and getting my timetable and so on, I retreated to the students union and the campus with Ginny. Everyone else seemed to have lots of friends and I got the feeling she would rather have been hanging out with her fellow students from Biochemistry than looking around with me. I felt as uncool as a Morris Dancer at a rave.

Ginny lived over on the Wirral with her parents so she didn't have the 'fish out of water' problems that I was encountering – after a day in Liverpool she could go home to her mum's amazing cooking and her own familiar room. Still, we explored the campus together and visited places like the adjacent Catholic Cathedral where there was a café.

Somehow or other we always ended up back at my room in the afternoons and indulged in some youthful shagging. As with all of that kind of thing I can't remember anything except that my single bed was very small and that in retrospect I didn't realise that Ginny was breaking a central tenant of her Christian faith by letting me have my wicked way. In my defence, she seemed to enjoy the physicality as much as I did.

At this point, I should mention that I think that I must have already been up to the Wirral during the summer, where she lived in middle-class Thornton Hough. Also, as I mentioned in the first instalment of my life story that she visited me in Devon before my A levels were over. How the mighty were fallen – me that is. I was no longer the hard-working boy with an addiction for finishing first in exams, but now the person who put seeing his girlfriend before revising for his final Physics A level exam? I say girlfriend when I didn't actually consider us as a pair. With Ginny I was always on my toes and as insecure as a midget at an orgy. To me, Ginny was as comprehensible as Nuclear Physics and as high maintenance as an F1 racing car. I'm not blaming her for either but the inescapable truth was that I had more chance of playing for Liverpool than meeting her deepest emotional needs.

In Dawlish she'd stayed next door which was a hotel at the time. I don't know what mum thought of her except that in one unguarded moment she had diplomatically opined that Ginny was 'posh'. The two of us never consummated our relationship then – but not from want of trying. I think I said to Rog that how men and women ever had it off was beyond me. Ginny seemed confused as well and we were left sticky and frustrated on many occasions.

One of the only other incidents from her stay that I can remember was during a walk up to work at Radfords (Terry didn't mind me bringing her along). At some point she revealed that she was a Christian and asked me what I thought of the whole committing your life to Jesus thing. At the time I didn't know there was any difference between churchgoers and Christians but because I respected her intellectually, I accepted her explanation that there was one. After that I guess the subject was dropped although she'd planted a seed that would germinate years later.

Returning to the thorny or, perhaps, horny issue of sex, we managed it for the first time that summer in her bedroom. Youthful ardour had brought us close to the magic moment on many previous occasions but this time, with the help of some Vaseline, we succeeded. It was actually a bit of a surprise when it happened and because we were so conditioned to failure, I don't think either of us were immediately convinced. When we realised that our genitals were actually engaged, however, surprise rather than lust was the overriding emotion of the moment.

After that it seemed so much easier and, as you might expect, we practised a lot. There were difficulties of course - avoiding pregnancy and unexpected entrances into her room by her mother being the chief areas of concern. But we succeeded in avoided both embarrassing scenarios so hats off to us. Of course, I didn't realise it at the time but, leaving aside the possibility of Ginny's mum discovering us enthusiastically copulating, I suppose there must have been a tension for Ginny between her Christian faith and what she got up to with me. I wasn't weighed down by any such moral considerations: as far as I was concerned I loved her and couldn't see beyond that. In fact I regarded the sex before marriage debate as open and shut as the theory of evolution. My friends and I didn't see a moral dilemma: we all agreed that shagging before marriage was just dandy.

Later, Rog and I caught up with each other and shared our first-time-shagging experiences. Unlike me, for Rog everything went perfectly and he told me later that he'd wondered how the hell I could have messed up so many times. Until on a later occasion he too fell victim to the unwilling cock syndrome and knew exactly what I meant. We both agreed that stopping to think about what one was doing was fatal!

Where was I – oh yes in my first term at Liverpool with Ginny. Except the 'with Ginny' part didn't last for long. Yes, you guessed it – I chose Liverpool University because of a woman and within weeks that woman had decided I was cramping her style. For the life of me I don't remember the specifics of when she dumped me but she did after only a matter of weeks. Maybe it was a choice between me and God and the non-existent supreme being triumphed? Or perhaps I was the most boring man in Liverpool and she had a sadistic streak that I had a knack of revealing? And maybe I wasn't as good at shagging as I thought I was?

I'd like to say that I took it in my stride and embarked on three years of womanising, but I'm afraid the Chris Grayling of the nineteen seventies was a more delicate soul than he is today. In addition, I knew very little about women and relationships: I just didn't do one night stands or freestyle shagging so, thanks to Diana Rigg, it was either love or nothing. And that, my friends, is a recipe for a long protracted depression.

Looking back I can see that Ginny and I were bad for each other: for whatever reason, she always seemed to be annoyed with me and I was certainly incapable of meeting her emotional needs. She unerringly made me feel uncomfortable in my own skin: I wasn't a complete idiot but she made me feel like one. So when she finished with me I should really have rejoiced. Instead I went to pieces and spent the rest of the academic year in a state of melancholy, hoping against hope that Ginny would take me back.

In her defence Ginny wasn't a masochist, just a normal young woman. Apart from God, she introduced me to Tolkien and the Joni Mitchell Court and Spark album which was the soundtrack of my university years. I'm grateful to her for all three, even if the first didn't endure. Women were still a mystery to me back then and Ginny was the deepest and most perplexing of them all.

There were other things to be pissed off about as well, paramount of which was my academic progress. During that first term I did very little homework partly because I spent a lot of my thinking time fixating on Ginny. Mostly, however, it was because I didn't have a clue what the fuck my lecturers were going on about. In the lectures themselves everything made almost perfect sense, but afterwards when I looked at my notes they were as incomprehensible as ancient Sumerian. There was also so much of it – I reckon we covered material equivalent to an A level every week.

I sat in the maths department classrooms or the physics lecture theatres near the back with similar no-hopers. The ones I can remember were John Codd who never washed himself or his clothes and as the term progressed smelt more and more like a decaying dog turd. He did no work at all and only seemed to come to the lectures as a change from lying in bed. Another John, a Geordie, was tall and very clever but also did nothing. Tony Card, an Anglican, showed up occasionally, but doing any homework was apparently not high up on his list of priorities. Maybe he expected Jesus to sort out his exams for him when the time came? I also remember a couple of scousers, an older ex-army bloke and an albino arse-wipe sort who joined in with the rest of us on the back row with our collective looks of incredulity. The albino later got a First so was clearly a wanker pretending to know less than he did – or a genius.

So maths was turning out to be hard. Not only that - there was an awful lot of it. Proving the simplest concepts seemed to delight our lecturers while we sat there utterly clueless. I bought the core textbook for the course entitled 'Analysis' and never understood a word of it. The two scousers, Big John and I would often sit in a pub marvelling at the stupidity of the subject we had chosen to study.

At this point I should also add that one of the academic staff, a Dr Jim Message, was assigned as my tutor while I was an undergraduate. I only saw him a couple of times because asking him for help was out of the question: I sensed that that wasn't what he was there for and, anyway, my knowledge was so laughably insubstantial that going to him with a problem would have just been embarrassing. Dr Message was an austere, shy man who had probably looked about fifty since he was twenty. He was tall with a full head of grey hair and a stooping gait that was vaguely reminiscent of cross between Quasi modo and the BFG. He was clearly very clever – someone told me and the others that he was the first person to prove that the Earth's orbit was actually stable which seemed like a big deal to me.

Dr Message took me and his two other tutees out for dinner at a posh restaurant somewhere down by the Mersey during the first term. It was one of those evenings that we all had to reluctantly attend but it was, nevertheless, okay. Jim Message was both shy and kindly and I warmed to him. The few other times I actually plucked up the courage to try and find him in his office up on the fifth floor of the mathematics building ended in failure. He was out, probably combining research with avoiding any contact with students. Who could blame him?

I did try to work in my room at Morton every night – really I did – but it nearly always ended with nothing being achieved. I'd start off by reading a text book at my desk but after about ten minutes when it got unbearably boring I'd take it onto the bed and continue to look at it with my head resting on one hand. A couple of hours later I'd wake up *in* bed and it was time to go over to the Carnatic bar. I'd often see Big John there and we'd end up back in his room smoking and bemoaning our lot in life. I'd stagger home between two and three in the morning cursing Ginny and vowing to do some work the next day.

Anyway, near the end of term came the time for some exams. I had three: pure maths, applied maths and physics for which I scored 17%, 59% and 17% respectively. The two seventeens were an accurate representation of the fact that I had learned fuck all from my lectures since I'd arrived in Liverpool and obviously hadn't worked hard enough. I think I gained the 59% on the back of what I already knew from my A levels. I had to see someone because I had done so badly – in this case Dr Message – to be given a dressing down for my lack of progress. If I'm honest, however, I felt that I had let him down more than anything so his rather apologetic reading of the riot act stirred more guilt than fear into me.

The fact was that I needed three marks of at least 34% in the summer examinations to stay on at Liverpool so I had to double my scores in two of the subjects by then. The die was cast.

2: January to June 1975

When I came back to Liverpool in January my main aim was to work. I needed to get the marks necessary to stay on at university because the thought of failure was too painful to think about How hard could it be? Very difficult actually – after spending the first term without doing any work, getting up to speed was like running a hundred metres race in a gorilla outfit – you were never going to win and there'd be a lot of unnecessary sweating. Even qualifying for the next round – in this case another year studying maths - was going to be tough.

My friends to a man were a bad influence in so far as none of them had ever knowingly read a sentence of a textbook. Big John and John Codd continued to treat university like a Butlin's holiday camp, albeit where the latter was concerned, without the showers. On the other hand, Tony Card got his act together with about three weeks to go before the summer exams. He obviously realised that it was down to him rather than God to make an effort.

I still saw a lot of Big John - he played the tin whistle as Geordies do, and he introduced me to the folk club scene in Liverpool. We still spent many late nights in his room smoking and putting the world to rights. I can't remember his surname and such are the idiosyncrasies of memory that two of my most vivid recollections of him are of his descriptions of a black dump he'd made after drinking eight pints of Guinness and of another occasion when he was sick out of the window of his room.

Clearly he and the other John had other priorities rather than passing any exams and neither of them possessed my innate fear of failure. I didn't admit it at the time but I also didn't want to let my mum down – it didn't seem fair that she would have to suffer the consequences of my self-inflicted stupidity.

Studying maths at university was, for me at least, excruciatingly difficult. Whereas A level maths was fine if you did a sensible amount of work, I never quite understood what I was doing during my degree course. I spent many fruitless hours in the Harold Cohen Library and in my room pouring over my notes and the recommended texts. Really I should have got hold of some past papers and focussed on them. Instead I tried to learn the subjects I was studying from scratch. And, as I mentioned above, I received no guidance from anybody.

In those days, apart from the December exams, the maths department at Liverpool did very little monitoring of my progress. Yes, Jim Message delivered a rather apologetic bollocking, but that was it. So I got on with it on my own and, to cut a long story short, I just about passed the summer exams and I was allowed back to continue with my studies for another year. I wasn't surprised that both Johns didn't reappear in October so God knows where their lives took them after that. Tony Card, however, did, so a combination of cramming and his spiritual connections were apparently enough.

You might also be asking yourself what else I got up to in those two terms. Well, apart from trying to catch up academically after giving everybody else a term's start and moping about Ginny, not a lot really. Being a student is to live in a kind of bubble so I can't say I got to know any Liverpudlians at all. Yes, the city felt exciting and different compared to the sleepy environment that I was used to, but I mostly stayed apart from it all. My life revolved around the university and not the city: I hardly read a newspaper and didn't watch the TV for the whole ten weeks of term. I listened to the local radio station, Radio City, but back then I wasn't really a political animal.

At that stage of my emotional development it almost goes without saying that I dreamt of getting back with Ginny. I was romantic in the worst possible meaning of the word – I equated my own longing and unrequited love with a reality that is mostly only found in Hollywood or Barbara Cartland novels. I needed a kindly male to give me mature advice and they are rarer than Tottenham league title wins.   I think there was the odd occasional rekindling of my relationship with Ginny but I can't really remember. I certainly didn't have eyes for anyone else.

It is also worth mentioning that communications were on a whole different level back then. Now, everyone is only a text or a call away on a mobile, but not in 1975. I actually received correspondence in my pigeon hole and Mum and I wrote to each other every week. So if I did see Ginny, fuck knows how we arranged it. As I also mentioned in my previous book, mum always phoned me from a call box every week. She'd ring the public payphone next to B Block's entrance and someone would answer it and come up to the top floor to get me to run downstairs to speak to her.

The only vivid memory that I still have regarding Ginny is of a warm sunny day after the exams. For some incomprehensible reason I went over to the Wirral and Thornton Hough and some town that could have been Bebington or Birkenhead. I know why I went – it was on the off and very unlikely chance that I would see Ginny. Perhaps I needed to draw a metaphorical line in the sand so that I could start my life again without her? All I can remember is that Boris Becker was playing on centre court at Wimbledon and he was on the screens of the televisions I passed in some shop windows.

It would have probably been more beneficial to engage the services of a decent psychiatrist. Of course I didn't see her: I smoked too much and eventually gave up and went back to Carnatic feeling idiotic. In one sense, however, it was the end of a very long goodbye. I was done and I would never again revisit the kind of extended unhappiness she had put me through.

So far as sport was concerned I still played badminton. I'd decided to give up football at university and concentrate on the racket sport – one of many poor decisions I've made over the course of a lifetime. It's not that I could have played football for the university you understand – it's just that badminton has probably caused most of my joint problems in later life and wasn't particularly enjoyable at the time anyway. That's probably why most non-sporty men and women are still going strong into their seventies and beyond, while people like me have to fight against osteoarthritis and joint replacements and general knackeredness.

In Freshers' Week I went along to the sports centre and signed up. It was a big surprise to see that Mike Finnegan, a medic in his second year, was the captain of the club. We had history - he was the Devon singles champion back in the day when Rog, Bill and I used to compete down in Torquay every year. He and his mates came from Plymouth and were probably better coached (we did everything from books if you can call that coaching). He happily put me into the first team which probably indicates that he thought that I was better than I actually was.

I could cope with the first team when I had a good partner but I hardly ever seemed to have one during my three years at Liverpool (they probably felt the same way about me). All of the memories from that year are grim: both the tournaments we entered that year: the English and British University tournaments at Crystal Palace and Bath respectively, resulted in round one defeats and the North West UAU team event wasn't much better. The only time I had a good partner was when Tan Whatever from Malaysia came out of retirement and basically ripped our opponents to shreds while I stood at the net trying to look useful. It was a bit like the time I reluctantly agreed to play a match for Invicta in Tunbridge Wells the day after I'd had my vasectomy. I'd only said 'Yes' on condition that my partner Andy Witton did all the running while I wore three pairs of tight underpants and played like a man who'd recently been kicked in the balls.

One of my first experiences of the badminton club was of a local league match in Bootle. In order to get home we had to walk around Queens Drive, the city ring road, before getting a lift from a taxi. We were walking for hours and I got in very late. Looking back, if I had my time over again, I would have walked away from the sport back then and spared myself the arthritic knee and hip I developed in my fifties. So here's some advice people – if you don't want to wear out your joints give most sports a miss when you're young - you're better off just running or going to the gym.

In those days anyone could go along to a First Division football match, pay at the turnstiles and go in and watch. Even in Devon the Liverpool Kop was legendary so I went along a couple of times on my own and stood to see Liverpool. It is a sobering thought that Bill Shankly was still the Liverpool manager in 1974. Going to a live match for the first time, it struck me how different the experience was to watching one on the telly and how Kevin Keegan really was Liverpool's star player - the ball always seem to be at his feet. I saw them draw 2 – 2 with Derby County, the soon to be champions, and even I could see that Clough's men were a good team.

Liverpool city centre was a world apart from what I was used to in Devon. The shops were bigger - George Henry Lee and Lewis's, for example, were huge department stores, and on Saturday it got incredibly crowded. I'd never experienced anything like it and avoided going downtown in the future because the experience really was so uncomfortable. I also got to know Sefton Park and the walk into the university via the park, Princess Ave and the ethnic Granby Street area. Sometimes I walked down to Smithdown Road past the suburban looking Penny Lane and did it that way. Liverpool still seemed like an alien place to me and I looked forward to going home in the summer.

Apart from all of the above I also gradually got used to living in Morton House, one of the Carnatic halls of residence with its thousand-plus students. Morton and Lady Mountfield Houses were set on the other side of the huge site from the others and only a few hundred metres up from Sefton Park which I sometimes ran around to keep fit. It was three miles and in those days that was relatively easy.

The boys on my floor were pleasant and unobtrusive enough. So anonymous in fact that I hardly remember any of them. Below us was a floor of girls, all of whom were, as far as I was concerned, unremarkable. On the ground floor were a gang of boys, less amenable than us but still friendly enough. I don't think we had much to do with each other so they could have had nightly sessions of gay group sex and I wouldn't have known.

Gradually Morton became more and more familiar and after a year I thought of it as home.

3: The Summer of 1975

Spending the summer holidays in Dawlish, which were all of July, August and September and most of June except for a brief visit to Liverpool to get my results and make that day trip to the Wirral, was no hardship at all. If my memory serves me correctly, Rog and I washed up at Radfords Hotel for Terry Crump (it's in *Diana Rigg...*). We also saw each other regularly in order to socialise or play badminton at the club. We even hired a court to train against each other a couple of times a week.

By then Rog's circle of friends was different to mine insofar as he still mingled with old acquaintances from Torquay Technical College while I knew no old students from Teignmouth Grammar. Bill was heavily involved with his new girlfriend Beverly, and the running joke was that he spent too much time with her. In fact all of the time.

If you remember, John, the fourth member of our gang, had gone away to sea to work on the QE2. He did come back at least once and we all went out for a drink somewhere, Bill inevitably getting pissed and throwing up back at John's parents place which was now on the Exeter Road. I was also a bit tipsy but Roger told me afterwards that John had squeezed some of Bill's vomit back into the latter's drinking glass because he was damned if he was going to waste good alcohol. How the pair of us laughed afterwards and unless Bill reads this, he will never know. Come to think of it, that may have all happened while I was doing A levels and the other two were at Torquay Technical College. It did happen though and when I showed this to Rog he said:

Yes – all true. I remember it as first year A level time. I still had my old A30 which John Pitcher laid in front of in the main road to stop me driving, so I went up on the wide pavement and drove along there for a few yards – until John appeared from somewhere and laid on my bonnet before bending my coat hanger radio aerial in half. John had bought the Bacardi on the QE2 and didn't want to waste it. He figured it had only been in Bill's stomach for less than 5 minutes. But I couldn't believe it when he rang the cloth out into Bill's glass. I could see flecks in it, but Bill was so pickled he could hardly see the bloody glass let alone what was in it!

Rog also saw John again when I wasn't around – in fact that time at his house was the last time I ever saw him. According to Rog, John told him how he lost his virginity to a hooker. He sent me this:

Apparently she said to her old man, "I'm just popping down to the garden shed with this bloke (John), watch the chips will yer, I won't be long" John said she was as dry as a Nun's fanny and that he had to push like Geoff Capes with electrodes on his balls , to try and get in. He said he couldn't pull his foreskin back into place for two weeks afterwards!

Back to my story…

As I mentioned in *Diana Rigg…* the highlight back then of Rog's and my week was the football match between staff and guests from Radfords Hotel on Thursday evenings after work. Those were the days when, whatever the time of day or state of my health, I could enjoy the thrill of playing football. After the match we would all go back to the Rockstone Hotel bar with the guests where, once or twice, I got terribly drunk. My unfortunate experience with Bacardi is also referenced in the other book. Happy days.

Sometime in late July or August my solitary days without a girlfriend were about to end. Once or twice on my walk up to work at Radfords I passed a very attractive girl walking a dog. I recognised her from Teignmouth Grammar and we smiled at each other in recognition. Somehow or other I found out that she liked me, I asked her out and, even more amazingly, she said 'Yes'!

It was the start of a relationship that lasted for more than two years. Martine, or Teeny as she was known to everyone, was much younger than me but I wasn't complaining because she was gorgeous. She was still at school and her dark, exotic beauty captivated my mum who was just as shallow as I was. Apparently, Teeny had fancied me when I was still at Teignmouth and I had a vague memory of her and a friend watching me play football, oblivious to her unrequited love and my undeserved good fortune to be the object of her affections. That summer, her mum and step dad moved into a large, detached house no more than 150 metres from our flat and, after that, it wasn't long before I saw her taking the family dog Bonzo for a walk.

My mum wasn't unique in liking Teeny: everybody loved her. Terry and the Italian staff at Radfords looked at her adoringly and must have wondered which drugs I'd used to persuade her to go out with me. She was dark with a lovely open face. When she smiled all the men took a deep breath and all the women probably came over a bit weird themselves. Why she was enamoured of me, God only knows, but she was, and looking back, I wish I'd realised how lucky I was at the time. I don't think I treated her badly - that's just not the way I am - unless you count lack of empathy and sensitivity as abuse - but I suspect I may have taken her for granted more than I should have. She was the perfect girlfriend and I was almost the perfect loser and should have realised. Instead, I gave off the impression that she was just as lucky to be going out with me as I was to be going out with her when clearly that was absolute bollocks. I was batting out of my league back then but I didn't realise. And it's too late to say sorry now because I lost contact with her over 40 years ago.

With Teeny in my life, the rest of the summer flew by. When she was on her long school summer holiday I would see her in the afternoons when we would occasionally sunbathe, take Bonzo for a walk or make love in her bedroom. At night we'd perfected the process of sneaking into her bedroom while her parents were asleep and having sex before I climbed out of the window and jumped down to the ground outside and headed off home. Nowadays I would have needed drugs for one and a ladder for the other.

Rog also had a regular girlfriend by now. Cindy was a local girl, beautiful and outspoken enough to be my equal in in that sense. She was also able to make Teeny laugh and the three or four year age difference between them didn't seem to matter. The four of us would go to the football match every week and the two girls would watch from the side-lines and come back to the pub afterwards with us. Believe it or not they also accompanied us to badminton matches.

If you thought badminton was a winter sport then you clearly hadn't heard of John Underhill and his aged mother who had started something called The Teign-Daw Wanderers. Membership was by invitation only and I don't know how we got involved with him but we did. John and his adoring mater arranged numerous matches around the county for us to go to. Cindy and Teeny would often accompany us in Rog's car and while we were on court they would watch and talk amongst themselves. When we were in between games, we would all either go to the pub or joke, probably at John's expense or his poor partner, with them in the hall as we watched. The other men from our team or the opposition would gaze at Cindy and Teeny adoringly. I don't know about Rog, but I took it all for granted.

A word about John - he was a gangling bachelor of about 40 with a drooping moustache, skinny legs and a habit of wearing wristbands and headbands when he was playing. Apart from his mother he probably never spoke to another woman except when Cindy and Teeny were at the matches. If they made Channel 4 documentaries back then he would have made the perfect subject for one: God knows if he had other hobbies apart from playing badminton but if he did they had to be weird ones. We speculated that he'd only ever slept with a badminton racket or a teddy bear and the jury was out on whether he'd discovered masturbation although Rog pointed out that:

Strange – cos I remember a lot of people calling him a wanker! He used to keep looking over to his mum after every shot. She would nod at him and continue knitting him his next sweater. They were always too big and reached down to his knobbly knees. He was very selective about our opponents – they were usually members of the local blind school or some other poor bastards that he could smash into oblivion. Anything to get his mum's nod. Do you remember the team badges that she made and handed out to us with such pride? I don't know how you kept a straight face when you received yours and said it was something you would always treasure! They had bits of felt cut out in the image of a strangled goose doing a shit on the pavement. A far cry from the Dawlish Black Swan on The Brook that it was meant to be.

Although we moaned about John and his mum behind his back and especially about the ridiculous matches that they arranged, we still invariably said 'Yes' to playing in them when we were asked us to play. There was a kind of masochistic pleasure in visiting far flung places in Devon, especially with the girls in tow. When John was on court he would occasionally glance in our direction for encouragement and Rog or I would nod approvingly. While we were on court we ourselves had developed a fun game called 'Playtime' where we would deliberately extend the rallies against weaker opponents just to make them run.

On one memorable night we succeeded so well that one man ran through the open door at the side of his court because of his increasing side-to-side momentum.

Rog again:

Well remembered – it comes back to me now. He literally slammed through the doors at the side. I don't think we him saw again!

(And in case you think I've gone gaga I have eventually realised that the stuff about Cindy and Teign Daw Wanderers is also in *Diana Rigg*...)

Anyway, October soon came around and it was time to leave everyone and head back up north.

4: October 1975 to September 1976

Like all non-freshers I suppose that when I went back to Liverpool to start my second year I was a much more confident individual than I had been 12 months previously. Of course all of that is relative - I was still a pillock - but that didn't stop me thinking that I was a mature and experienced undergraduate. Going out with Teeny must have also boosted my self-esteem: having someone think you're special has that effect. I was still a dick, and subconsciously thought, quite misguidedly, that I deserved an attractive lover. Maybe deep down I couldn't quite believe that I had an incredibly cute and loyal girlfriend in Devon but it was a reassuring thought and lent me some undeserved self-confidence. I went home every three weeks or so to see her but apart from that all I had to do was work hard and have fun: how hard could that be?

As you might have guessed - I was still in B Block at Morton House. After all, moving out required initiative and friends: Ginny had deprived me of the former and I was never really likeable enough for other people to actually want to live with me. Besides, I liked clean showers and toilets and a rodent-free living environment, rather than a dirty, ramshackle house down some Liverpudlian backstreet. And, even though Carnatic food was pretty terrible, at least I never had to spend time preparing it.

This is probably a good time to also mention B Block's top floor cleaner, June, a cheerful, bright motherly scouser. We hit it off famously: I've always had a knack of getting on with older women. I soon began to think of her as my surrogate mother in Liverpool and we would always have a gossip if I was ever around in the mornings when she was in B Block.

There were also a new bunch of first years on my floor. Nearly all of the ones from my own first year had moved on to pastures new apart from, if I remember correctly, some annoying oik of a Lancastrian engineer called John. Fortunately, he kept himself to himself, because when he did come out he really was the most boring and irritating student alive. Of course, he probably felt exactly the same way about me.

In the room next to me now was a flame-headed ultra-confident sort called Terry Gilligan. He was like Bill of old in that he had a stutter but that was where the similarity ended. He was good-looking and knew it: girls were putty in his hands and as far as I can tell he put those hands to great use during his time at Liverpool. He was, as far as I was concerned, likeable and unlikable in equal measure and over the couple of years I knew him we had to endure some mutual alpha male loathing of each other. He was definitely the only person I came close to hitting while I was at university.

Terry apart, there was Bob Edwards from Aberystwyth, bespectacled and permanently grinning. A medic, and as left wing as Billy Bragg. He's now a retired GP living on the Wirral and after a long lull we now stay in reasonably regular contact via Zoom. When I decided to write this I asked him if he had any memories from our time at Liverpool and he came up with a few. He's one of only two people from my undergraduate days that I'm still in contact with so hats off to him for his patience!

Bob's first attempt at remembering his freshers year at Liverpool included recollecting his shyness and naivety when he first arrived at Morton. Apparently he stayed in his room for six weeks to begin with but after that he became an intrinsic part of the gang and the man I did most with while we were at Morton together. I really liked him even if he always beat me whenever we went for a run around Sefton Park!

He also says he remembers going over to the Wirral with me and a few others to pop in on Ginny, so it seems that I wasn't over her even then. In my defence I didn't remember that at all. More of Bob later.

There was also Viv Barclay from North Wales, eighteen going on fifty-three and the kind of man who would talk to anybody and usually did. Completing my new gang of friends was Pete Blurton whose dad was a vice president of some division of ICI. It's hard to believe now, but back then ICI was probably the biggest industrial company in the country and seemingly as permanent as Woolworths. Looking back dispels the myth that 'forever' means forever - both companies are now gone, swept away by our own modern age. Pete, a Yorkshire man, was clearly from a more middle-class background than Bob, Viv, Terry or I, but having said that he really was a nice guy.

For that year we did everything at hall together - going over to dinner at Carnatic Hall at six and the bar at about 9 or 10 every night. We also got into the habit of playing cards after dinner every night in someone's room. It was usually just a round of contract whist before we went back to our own rooms to work until it was time to go to the bar. Bob and I always played and the latter was the only one ever to succeed in fulfilling all thirteen contracts in a game. We named it a 'Bobby' in his honour.

I had a happy year I suppose even if the mathematics was as impenetrable as always. I still hadn't realised that I needed to pass exams and not learn, for example, Topology from scratch. The only exam that I remembered going well was Jim Message's Classical Mechanics paper and he congratulated me when I had to face a board of lecturers after the results. I could tell the others on the panel didn't share Dr Message's view of my mathematical prowess.

Bob and I teamed up to go to various football matches and concerts. He loved his music and was up for any adventure involving Anfield or the Liverpool Empire. Teeny came up to visit once and wowed everybody. It's difficult to believe but we managed to sleep on my narrow single bed together for a few nights.

Luckily, none of my examination results counted towards my degree, so when I scraped through again in the summer there was still all to play for the following year. Tony Card continued to survive on three weeks work per annum. On the subject of religion I think it was about then that an interest in God began to stir within me. Fuck knows, I was an irritating prick even without that, but I was headed for Morton House CU and would become a fully indoctrinated activist in the future. It's a miracle, even in the Biblical sense, that I still have any friends left from those times.

When I went home for the summer, the weather in that legendary year of 1976 was something people of my age will always remember. Every day, and I mean every day, was unfailingly sunny. You could rely on it like you can in, for example, Spain every year. Of course, a Minister for Drought was appointed in late August thereupon it started to rain and hardly stopped thereafter. The public were even advised by politicians on the telly to share a bath which, thank God, nobody took seriously.

Having said all of that I can't remember many of the specifics of those months. I'm sure I saw a lot of Teeny and I know that she and I went out with Rog and Cindy many times. There must have also been a lot of badminton played, mostly for *The Wanderers* and, of course, I was still working at Terry Crump's although I might have been promoted to the bar by then. I say promoted when moved is probably a better description. As I mentioned in *Diana Rigg...,* Rog, who had left by now, and I always used to row with the Italian waiters when we washed up, so maybe Terry and Janet decided to find a less confrontational role for me to occupy. Years afterwards Janet confided to me that sacking me was never an option so it is to Terry and Janet I still owe a debt of gratitude for putting up with my obnoxious behaviour.

At some point either this summer or previously, Terry became interested in horse riding. Well, I say "interested", but where Terry was concerned, obsession is probably a better way of describing his interest in any of his hobbies. Whichever summer it was when the bug bit him, somehow Rog and I also went on his trips up to Haytor on Dartmoor where we went out in a posse for an hour or two, riding on a rag-tag bunch of equestrian horseflesh.

Even if Rog and I weren't very good we were always keen to gain a new skill, however painful the learning process. We made a habit of falling off horses whether they were walking, trotting, cantering or even galloping across the moors. It was the subtle changes in direction that always got us and we were often the cause of many bouts of uncontrollable laughing. It's amazing that neither of us were hurt because a horse is a big animal to dismount from when it's moving at speed - now I risk serious injury when just falling over in the garden. Back then, however, I was deposited in gorse bushes, projected over my mount's head and dropped on my back and never felt a thing. Maybe we were always relaxed when we hit the ground and therefore escaped any injury? Once we even fell off simultaneously, both fearing the other's cutting comments as we stood up, only to find the other staggering gingerly to his feet.

Rog remembers that one:

I was on that bastard little horse called Rowen, whose mission was to eject her rider, i.e. me, into outer space as quick as possible. She succeeded and I landed rather hard, a granite rock breaking my fall. I smashed my nose, which is still crocked to this day, and I bled like a stuck pig. Kenny* lent me his handkerchief which was freshly laundered and pressed (just like his underpants). He never asked for it back – no wonder, it was like a crisp dried blood and snot.

*Ken Martin – a great bloke a couple of years older than us who joined in with badminton and Terry Crump related activities. Not one of the gang but unfailingly friendly and positive. He died in 2021.

Rog and I also recently figured out that this was the summer that Bill and Bev tied the knot down in the Registry Office in Torquay. All four of us went, of course, and I was a very forgettable best man. So forgettable in fact that hardly any of the day remains in my memory banks. Even Rog, when I asked him about it, and who can remember details of past events that have long departed my consciousness, thought the wedding took place in 1975. Even though my mind was blank regarding the whole day I knew it had to be 1976 because I had a photograph of Teeny and me from it and she wasn't around enough in the summer of '75 to be there.

Basically, I guess 1976 was just an idyllic summer which I took for granted. The only other thing of note that I can remember is going to the Lake District with Rog and Cindy and Teeny in Rog's Cortina. I still have a photograph of us standing by the car outside the hotel where we stayed. I've never before noticed how pissed off Teeny looks in it so it can't have been much fun for her. The weather was also breaking but it was still largely dry, even in September. It was mostly fun but I can remember disagreements with Cindy because, quite rightly, she thought that students had too much free time and wanted to make the most of her one week away. Rog is naturally a peacemaker but he couldn't stop me rubbing Cindy up the wrong way with my lack of diplomacy.

When I showed him this he said:

I remember she wanted to always be in the front and never offered you two a turn. In hind sight I should have stepped in – but then again, missing out on a shag that night was too big a price to pay!

And (which I've obviously forgotten and he probably got wrong anyway...)

I remember you impressing the girls on our first evening meal together recounting a story of how you were fascinated that after having a shit there was always more piss in your cock when you stood up! I made a mental note to use that one myself next time I was out with a new girl!

Things between Teeny and I were okay I think but I did make her cry once on a walk because I am such an irritable bastard. I have a photograph of her looking upset with me on a mountain somewhere near Helvellyn and my behaviour probably also explains her demeanour in the photo with the others.

When it was time to leave Dawlish for my final year at Liverpool I was actually looking forward to seeing Bob and all the others again. Terry, Pete and he were coming back to Morton with me and I would soon meet Dave Peru and Mark Thompson who I eventually shared a flat with a few years later. I would also fall in love with my future wife, even if she didn't realise I had the hots for her until much later.

5: My Degree Year

I can honestly say that for all of my third year I worked as hard as I could towards my degree - hard but not smart. In fact, I'd been playing catch-up since the Christmas of my traumatic first year, so I never really felt totally on top of my studies. I just didn't know how to prepare for my finals – and no one was giving away any hints on how to master my courses either. And I'm not blaming Jim Message - or anyone else for that matter – I'm sure he would have helped me if he could but it was difficult for me to own up to my level of stupidity to such a supremely gifted mathematician. I felt that he wouldn't be able to comprehend my own level of buffoonery.

And, on top of that, I had still had the rather quaint idea that if I was to become a graduate in the subject then I should have a thorough grasp of all of my courses. I can see now that that's an idiotic idea – I should have just asked for past papers and advice from everybody who knew anything about taking their finals.

Still, I really wanted a First, and without the strain of Ginny in my life, I was able to focus on my academic objectives. Except that's easier said than done when you're on your own. Not knowing how to tackle my revision was one thing, but the other was finding the energy to work intelligently and hard enough. Every evening in my room at Morton, after cards with Bob et al, I would enact the desk, bed, sleep routine before ending most evenings at the Carnatic Bar with Bob and the others. I just couldn't help myself and believe me I tried. Reading any kind of textbook is boring but my maths notes were a guaranteed knock-out!

During the day when there were no lectures I also spent hours in the Harold Cohen library, achieving little. Still, as May and the week of my finals approached I was reasonably confident that I would do okay. Since Easter there had been no lectures and I'd applied myself single-mindedly to my revision. I had the classic revision TT on the walls of my room and for the first few weeks I stuck to it. I know six hours doesn't sound much but they were all full-on.

In fact I would have kept to my six hours a day schedule for the whole six weeks except that my body intervened. At the start of the third week I sat down to study after breakfast and noticed that I had a headache. So I shut the folder and, hey presto, I noticed that I no longer had a headache. Tentatively, I opened the folder or whatever it was again and my headache returned instantly. This happened several times until I was forced to abandon my notes for a few days until I was physically able to sit in front of them without incurring pain. June thought it was hilarious when I told her.

At Morton things continued happily. As I said above, Bob, Terry and Pete were joined at the start of the autumn term by Dave Peru and Mark Thompson. Dave was a cool Londoner supposedly studying architecture and Mark, from North Wales, was doing Law.

The following year I would get to know Mark and Dave, especially the latter, a lot better but I can still remember liking Dave immediately. He was into music in a big way and we found that we both had a soft spot for Joni Mitchell, Paul Simon and others. I must have had a gift for getting on well with layabouts because Dave only seemed to work when an assignment was due. Then he would burn the midnight oil on the nights leading up to the hand in. He also smoked Benson and Hedges which gave us even more in common.

The big story of the year so far as Morton House was concerned was a short-lived feud with the ground floor lads who were much more boisterous than us. One night they came back to hall as pissed as farts and emptied the girls' tampon disposal bin in our corridor. There was probably other mischief going on as well but I forget it now. Anyway, I think this was the final straw, and we decided to get even.

Terry and I forged a letter from our House Tutor, a lady whose name I can't recall, asking the miscreants to visit her house on site one evening.

Bear in mind that this was in an era before printing and typing documents was as simple as it is today. The whole process took some planning: Terry and I had to compose said letter and type and print it in the Psychology Department where he was a student, before sneaking the letters, complete with the forged signature of the tutor, into the miscreants' pigeon holes in Morton's front office.

I remember vividly the four or five of us sitting in dinner that evening when the others came in. They must have received the letters and concluded they were in the shit because we had dobbed them in. They treated us to hard stares from the dinner queue as we sat together as straight-faced as a group of Taliban. We concentrated hard on eating, trying to avoid eye-contact as well as not giggling..

Later, back in Pete Blurton's room we watched out of his window as the entire bottom floor filed out of the exit, into a chilly winter's evening en route to the tutor's house. It was so funny I had to bite on my arm to control the volume of my laughter. We could only imagine the look of surprise on the tutor's face when a dozen contrite undergraduates came knocking on her door while she was oblivious to the fact as to why they were there.

To hand it to the downstairs gang, we all had a good laugh about it afterwards. They grudgingly admitted that we had pulled off an amazing practical joke. Apparently the tutor had invited them in for drinks and a chat without anyone knowing what the fuck was going on.

The only other time I remember crossing swords with the lads and girls from downstairs was on a Saturday evening in the summer. Some of us had gone down to the girls' kitchen where there was a large table and, God knows how, there was soon a game of strip contract whist going on. Three or four of the lads from downstairs were involved and soon most of us were virtually naked, our modesty only being kept alive by the tabletop. Wisely, none of the girls were involved in the game, but soon there was a crowd of onlookers huddled together in the kitchen.

One of the Lady Mountford blocks faced the kitchen as well and there were crowds of their students gathered at the windows cheering us on. Most of the interest was focused on the arse-cracks of the players that were visible through a perfectly positioned hole in the rear of the chairs as well as the bare legs and piles of clothes. I can't remember how it ended except for Bob's grinning face as the downstairs lot lost all of their clothes. Also the cheering from Lady Mountford and the incredulous looks of the female students whose kitchen we had hijacked.

Just before my finals I had a bit of bad luck – well a lot actually. I was in the shower on the Sunday afternoon before the day of my first finals exam when I noticed that one of my arms and, as far as I could see, some of my back had a kind of red rash on it. I felt fine and was going to ignore it, but to be on the safe side, I thought I'd show Bob who was now living in the room next to mine. After a cursory glance he said that he thought I had German measles which, although good from the point of view that I wasn't going to actually feel too under the weather, was potentially a disaster for any girl on the site who was unknowingly pregnant and caught it off me.

To cut a long story short I had to go into quarantine for a week – the week of my finals. I couldn't get out of it – not only because Bob knew but also because, for all my failings, I did have a social conscience. I had to spend the whole week in a room in sick bay on the Carnatic site. It was undoubtedly the most boring seven days of my life. I did all of my exams in the room and I hardly had anyone else to talk to. I remember vividly Bob, Terry and the others coming up to my window every night and commiserating with me before trotting off to the bar for a drink and some socialising.

Not only that, I knew after the first exam that I wasn't going to get a First. Instead of taking the paper slowly and finishing faster and better, the self-imposed pressure I'd put myself under turned my brain to mush. Other exams went well but I knew that they weren't going to be enough to save me. I must have taken it in my stride, however, because I remember accepting my fate with my usual fatalism. What could I do anyway?

So far as being a student was concerned I loved being in Liverpool. The independence and the excitement of living in a busy city was, as you might expect, great fun. Later on in life I became a teacher and the academic year never held as much appeal as when I was receiving rather than giving lessons. Not that lectures took up much of our time - yes we had more lectures to attend than a typical Arts student and there was a lot of academic work, but there was still plenty of time to socialise and generally be young, footloose and fancy free.

As I mentioned earlier, I went to Anfield several times, but the best match by a long way was in March when Bob and I met up at about six and got to the ground early so we could get into the Kop to watch the second leg of the European Cup Quarter Final against St Etienne. It was a great night in the swaying cyclone that was that stand back then, especially when David Fairclough rammed home the winner near the end and I found myself dancing with some random scouser. And I was an Arsenal fan!

Bob, Dave and I would also go to concerts at the Liverpool Empire where bands such as Genesis, The Kinks, Sailor and others played. Bob to this day still can't believe that he went to see Sailor but he was basically up for anything musical so it's not that surprising to me!

When the exams were over there were a few weeks' wait before I had to go into the maths building to see where my name was on the results board. I went home to Teeny and then came back to see what I'd got. These days I expect results are posted online to save one the traumatic experience of straining with a group of your fellow students to see how you all got on. But not back then – anyway I didn't care much. I must have been pretty confident because I started looking from the top of the list. When I saw that I had an Upper Second I felt relieved and happy. If you must know, despite my nagging whenever I saw him, Tony Card scraped a general degree which wasn't bad for someone who only ever seemed to work in the month of May.

Mum and Teeny came up to Liverpool for the degree ceremony in The Philharmonic Hall on Hope Street. I'd gone home after the exams and we all got a taxi down to the station in Dawlish together. Teeny looked a dream as she walked along The Villas to meet us. I remember the taxi driver taking a deep breath in when he saw her.

I don't remember much about the trip itself, even the ceremony, except for a trip to Blackpool with Teeny on a swelteringly hot day. I remember the beach at Blackpool being scattered with donkey shit and a rollercoaster ride with Teeny where I did all of the screaming.

So that seemed to be that. I'd applied to do an M. Sc. sometime after the exams but I didn't expect the application to come to anything. Previously in the Milk Round back in the Spring Term I'd had a couple of interviews with Nat West and the old Midland Bank. The first one was really pressurised while the second was more of an old-boy kind of chit chat, so it was a surprise when it was Nat West that came through with an offer to be on their graduate training programme. Later in the summer I think I went to a residential course as a part of my training. One way or another, however, I hoped against hope that I would be accepted on the Methods of Applied Maths M. Sc. course and, just as importantly, get a grant so that I could take it. I felt that I had unfinished business with maths as a subject.

6: Autumn 1977

So, after my degree, I came back to Dawlish fully expecting to start life as a Nat West banker in the autumn. That apart, I had no plans and no idea what the future would hold – I had the usual misplaced confidence possessed by most people that life would pan out okay. 'What will be will be', is a saying reserved for those who can't be bothered to get off their arses to try and influence events, and back then I was a fully paid up member of the club. As I've already mentioned, I'd applied for an M. Sc. course but that was a really long shot – honestly, it was where my heart was, but reality is reality after all.

I was still going out with Teeny and all seemed well on that front. She had done very well, being accepted on a Marks and Spencer's junior management training scheme for students who'd finished their A levels. I wasn't surprised because she was classy and charming and beautiful – all attributes that M and S thought that they themselves possessed. She would be starting in September.

I guess I thought we might get married – I'd spent my whole life going with the flow so why would I change the habit now? We were happy, or at least I thought we were, so in a parallel universe we're married, have a couple of kids and are growing old somewhere in the Home Counties. In the real world I can't find her anywhere on Facebook or elsewhere online. I don't even know what name she goes by now.

The summer went by with nothing out of the ordinary happening except that I must have come to some sort of decision about Teeny and my future. Teeny had found out she would be working in Poole in Dorset at the M&S there and I decided that I wanted to be with her indefinitely - perhaps I'd decided that it wasn't fair on Nat West to lead them on when I was really only interested in going back to Liverpool or being with Teeny. I'd like to think it was the latter reason, but I've always been a self-centred bastard so who knows? At some point I told the bank that I wanted to come off the training scheme and decided to apply for a job, ironically, and somewhat nonsensically, at a bank branch in Poole. My lack of imagination was up there with Bonzo's.

Teeny was shocked and I can remember her saying something along the lines of, 'You'd really do that for me?', which probably indicates she was as much surprised as well as touched by my action. Looking back I've no idea whether or not I was committed to following her or whether I was stalling just to find out about the M. Sc.

I can't remember the exact details of what happened, but in September I remember hitching a ride up to Poole and surprising her at the checkout at M&S later that day. Today I would have messaged her on my mobile but back then it really was a shock for her when I showed up.

We lived together in her new digs for only a few days before I got a letter from the university telling me that I'd been accepted on the M. Sc. course. In retrospect that must have put the tin lid on it for Teeny because, despite exhibiting as much regret as I could, I accepted the university's offer. When push came to shove I wanted to be in Liverpool – looking back, the attraction of the carefree student lifestyle rather than the maths was what was calling me. Within days I was at the accommodation offices at the university trying to find somewhere to live: it really is true that in the end we do what we want to do.

I'd arranged nothing on the accommodation front so I was at the back of the queue where that was concerned. My options were extremely limited and I was offered a bedsit that reflected my lack of planning – a room in a house at the end of a road called Long Lane, a mile or so from Carnatic. It was horrible – reached up a flight of stairs in a slummy, run-down Victorian house in an awful neighbourhood. The room itself required a lot of elbow grease to get it clean and even then it was tired and unpleasant. I felt instantly unhappy and missed B Block and my friends.

To cut a long story short, I was only there about a month. I did the best that I could with it –

spending the whole of the first week scrubbing off the filth of previous occupants and making a shot at living there. I hated returning to my lonely room after a day at the university so when the chance came to return to B Block I jumped at it.

June, who I'd visited at some point knew my situation and nabbed for me the vacant room of someone who'd left. Even better, Dave Peru and some other friends were still there and I remember that it felt like coming home when I moved back in.

And I needed some security – Teeny had finished with me a couple of weeks previously so I was as pissed off as a young person with no imagination can be. Looking back it was an amusing sequence of events which I have related to friends many times afterwards but getting her letter and acting impulsively straight afterwards heralded one of the worst days of my life. So bad, in fact, that it makes it funny.

If I remember correctly, two weeks after the start of term I'd gone back to Devon to play in a badminton tournament with Rog up in North Devon. Afterwards, he and Cindy were driving me home in his Cortina when Teeny must have come up in the conversation. I remember saying then that I'd decided that she was the girl for me and I hoped we could make a go of it in the future. Fast forward a couple of days to the bedsit in Long Lane and I'm coming in after a day at the university. There is a letter from Teeny waiting for me and in it she tells me but she doesn't love me anymore and it's over. She's found someone else – a Royal Marine who's so much better than me. And loving. If that wasn't enough, she spells out to me what a cunt I've been over the last few years which, although probably thoroughly deserved, was a touch on the gratuitous side of cruel.

In retrospect reading the letter was like being plunged unceremoniously into one of Joni's Court and Spark tracks. Suddenly I was back in the unsettling world of broken relationships and life on the edge. Before opening my post I was living in a false reality where I felt pleased with myself without any corroborating evidence. Afterwards, the truth of the paper thin boundary between feeling entitled to happiness and being lonely and wretched became absolutely crystal clear.

Or should have been – instead I was stunned and disbelieving. With Ginny, being chucked always felt like an inevitability, but where Teeny was concerned I'd had no inkling of her discontent with me and our relationship. It was my own lack of self-awareness together with that sense of disbelief that prompted me to get an early train the next day for Poole. I've no idea whether the train went via London or anywhere else for that matter but it was a long, long journey. By the time I made it down there it was already dark and I came out of the station and walked up the hill to her house. It was raining and miserable and I knocked on the door.

It was answered by her housemate who went and found Teeny, leaving me waiting on the doorstep. When she appeared I wasn't invited in - she stood peeping around the barely-ajar door at me while I probably uttered inane expressions of regret. I can't remember what was said but, suffice it to say, the lady wasn't for turning. Looking back, who the fuck could blame her? When I first received the letter I should have taken it on the chin and moved on. I just couldn't believe that I was as much of a dick as she had said I was.

Although I would have denied it at the time, maybe I only wanted to see her so she could admit that she'd only written the letter whilst temporarily insane and that I was really a cool dude? Anyway, she didn't and half an hour later I was on a train headed back up North, still emphatically in denial about the truth of my newly acquired singleness and my own idiocy. I don't think I've ever been more depressed. An all night train via Crewe only strengthened the depths of my despair. Having said all of that I survived and after a few weeks I was back in B Block with June, Dave and the others.

This seems like a good time to thank Teeny, somewhat belatedly, for giving me two of the happiest years of my life. She rebuilt my inner confidence after it had been destroyed by Ginny and was the best girlfriend a young man could ever hope for. I only wish I'd known at the time how lucky I was and acted accordingly.

7: Spring 1978

My life after Teeny started much more quickly than it did after Ginny. I was older I guess and Liverpool felt like home now. I enjoyed my course: an M. Sc. in Methods of Applied Mathematics, even if I found some of the material as mystifying as I had during my degree. There must have been other people on the course but I shared an office in the Maths building with Wing Leung and an English chap from Cambridge who drove an old VW Beetle. I can't remember the latter's name but suffice it to say that he was a very nice guy. It probably also goes without saying that Wing and he actually understood the maths we were doing whilst my grasp of the material was, at best, tenuous. I remember Wing trying in vain to explain some line integrals to me while I tried to keep a look of complete mystification out of my eyes.

At Morton, things were great and I felt at home. I saw June most mornings when she came in to clean and in the evenings Dave Peru and I would discuss things like politics, music, women and life in general while smoking each other's cigarettes.

Dave was as relaxed about life as a ginger cat on weed. As I've already mentioned, he was outrageously cool as well as being a student of life rather than architecture, the subject he was actually supposed to be studying. Our rooms were next to each other's and we got on famously – at least in so far as I remember. We also spent time with Mark Thompson, a genial Welsh giant who treated Dave and I with amused indulgence. He worked hard and had a girlfriend who visited him regularly – two attributes that were permanently missing from Dave's and my own life at the time.

I was also getting interested in Christianity. There was an active CU in Morton and I went along to a few meetings to see what it was all about. In part it was a reaction to what I saw as my own failed attempt to live life properly and a genuine desire to put things right. On the other hand, maybe those motives found some unspiritual encouragement by the presence of a foxy young woman from Norfolk in the group called Hilary.

If I were to be brutally honest I'd own up to noticing her the year before while I was doing my finals year but had passed on trying to get to know her for a number of reasons. Firstly I already had a girlfriend, secondly I had a lot of work to do and thirdly I wasn't a Christian. Yes, I knew that winning her over involved a revamping of my lifestyle and that, my friends, would have to wait.

'Not another fucking woman!' I hear you mutter. 'When is the sad bastard going to do something that isn't motivated by a pretty face?' Well, obviously I cannot say whether that's true or not, but there was no denying that Hilary's membership of the CU did engender a greater religious fervency in me than might otherwise have been apparent. Anyway, it was complicated: there was other competition for her affections: mostly from an Iranian with an expensive Ford Capri with whom she seemed to be close 'friends'.

There were also several male members of the CU who treated the women in any religious group as potential future spouses. Hilary had sex appeal so she was top of those particular charts. I was oblivious to all of these undertones because in the process of searching for God I'd taken on the belief that anyone who believed in him was as pure as driven snow. This remained my view for months, if not years, and I was as innocent of the hidden motives of my fellow Christians as it was possible to be. Anyway, so far as Hilary was concerned, all I could do was accept that, for now, I was way down the pecking order of men ready to tempt her into romance.

Academically I had one other matter to resolve – the M. Sc. was fifty percent assessed by exam and the remainder via a dissertation. Of course I had no fucking idea what to write mine about until I got lucky one day in the maths building. I happened to mention this problem to Jim Message while we were sharing a lift and he said that he had one or two things that I could have a look at for him. This was clearly the best offer I was going to get and as his subject was Dynamical Astronomy and seemingly an interesting subject, I immediately agreed to take him up on his offer.

There is probably a copy of my dissertation somewhere in the library at the University of Liverpool but I've none myself. It's like an embarrassing film - I'd rather ignore it than be faced with the toe-curling embarrassment that would inevitably be involved if I read it. For example, it had to be re-typed because, amongst other errors, I managed to spell the word environment incorrectly throughout the piece (I didn't know back then that it had an n in it...and I used the word a lot). Bad spelling apart, I was also only too aware that it wasn't very good. So after I handed it in, I managed to avoid Dr Message's feedback for weeks, sensing that it wasn't up to muster.

In the days before email this was an easy enough thing to do and I think it was well into the autumn before we met in the street - he on his bike and me trapped on the pavement. He gave me his customarily apologetic dressing down and I had to go and collect it from his office to rewrite it. I think it was on the resonant behaviour of two of the moons of Saturn: Mimas and Tethys are names that ring a bell but I'm past caring now. Note to self – things that seem important at the time fade into insignificance with the passing of decades.

But I'm getting ahead of myself: one test I did pass that term was my driving test. I used BSM in Liverpool and got on well with my instructor. Still, I never really thought that I'd pass and on the day of the test I couldn't have been more nervous if I'd been called up in a dream for a trial with Arsenal where I wasn't permitted to wear any kit during the game. My foot shook and so must my hands after all the cigarettes I'd smoked beforehand. Incredibly, however, I passed. I could have literally kissed the instructor, even with tongues, and I don't think I've ever gained as much satisfaction from passing an exam as I did that one. I'd previously failed my test twice when I was sixth former at Teignmouth - having to drive with someone else watching you was akin to masturbating in front of the class during form time and I just wasn't up to it.

So when I came home for the Easter break I wanted to buy a car. Don't ask me why – I just wanted wheels. Luckily Rog found out that there was an old Cortina for sale at a farm just outside Dawlish. He drove me over there in his own Cortina and after some half-hearted haggling I owned 'Kenya', FVX 938B. It was called Kenya because the guy selling it had family out there and had stuck the name above the windscreen which I didn't bother to remove for months.

Naturally it needed an MOT to be legal but in those days there was a garage at the bottom of Fire

Station Hill in Dawlish, where a friendly bloke I sort of knew got it through for another hundred quid or so. For the rest of the month's holiday all I did was work on the car, see Rog and Terry and the gang and go for runs. Those were the days when you could actually work on a car because it had things like points and sparking plugs that you could tinker with. There was also a great scrapyard out on the Exeter Road that I used to frequent, clambering around the rows of neatly stacked cars looking for things like old regulator boxes and other goodies. I used to work on it at the back of the house where there were some garages and a quiet space to work. My mum hardly saw me and soon the day came to take my navy blue Ford with the green bonnet back to university.

Rog was full of good driving advice but it was still a mission, I can tell you, driving up to Merseyside on the M5, M6 and M62 at no more than sixty mph and mostly in the slow lane. My right foot ached from keeping the accelerator depressed and back then making it to the end of the journey was an something of an achievement.

All I can remember happening when I arrived was Dave Peru saying something like, 'Bloody hell Chris, you look so fit!' which was down to my daily running rather than the new car.

Anyway, I had wheels for the first time. I think I took the car down to Liverpool city centre with much trepidation but, after I'd survived, I never worried about driving anywhere again. I think I also took Dave and some others for a jaunt over to, you guessed, The Wirral. The Wheatsheaf pub was just up the road from Ginny's place and I half hoped that I would see her. We didn't and all I can remember from that trip was Dave remarking that I drove very close to some walls. We laughed but, worryingly, I had no idea that I was cutting it so fine.

8: Summer 1978

The M. Sc. exams were less traumatic than those of my degree. For a start I wasn't trapped in sick bay and there were fewer to prepare for. God knows how many core subjects there were or, for that matter, how many courses I had to choose of my own volition. I think the latter must have included one on Dynamical Astronomy with Dr Jupp, a young Jim Message protégé and I'm certain I did something called Radiative Transfer with Tony Bridgeman. The latter seemed like a playboy more than a lecturer and I remember him because he gave me lots of past papers and spent a lot of time going through questions with me. God knows what Radiative Transfer even is but I know I aced the exam because of Tony.

The course was for a year so I wasn't done until the end of September. Near the end I thought it would be nice to do a Ph. D. I figured that most of life's prizes are transient but being called 'Doctor' would at least last for as long as I lived. Looking back, maybe I wanted tangible 'proof' that I was clever? Jim Message was open to the idea, probably because it would mean he would have a postgraduate student, but I also had to have the nod from Prof. Oldroyd, the head of department.

I remember going up to the latter's office to ask him and he being utterly charming. I'd never spoken to him before: my only contact had been seeing him, constantly beaming, when he came into the maths department common room when lecturers and postgraduate students were gathered for morning or afternoon coffee.

He went over to a filing cabinet to look up my file and I could see that when he found my exam results that he was less than impressed. A frown began to replace his customarily smiling demeanour. Before I could brace myself for a curt refusal I think he came upon my optional subject results, including Radiative Transfer. They must have saved me: he said something along the lines of (in a slightly surprised voice): 'You're actually quite good at applying your knowledge. Yes I'll recommend you for a grant.'

And that was it. If Prof. Oldroyd, aka 'the Father of Rheology', said it would be okay for me to do a Ph D it would be. BTW, 'Rheology' is the study of non-Newtonian fluid dynamics, whatever the fuck that is, and something the Liverpool maths department were renowned for because of Oldroyd, the other HOD Professor Crapper (I know, he really was shit hot) and others.

So my future was decided. Two more years at Liverpool and a new office with Nick Willis and another guy whose name I forget. In the office next door was Sean Swarbrick who ended up being a good friend and later worked at the Met Office in Bracknell.

Jim Message gave me one of his papers to look at as a possible jumping off point into a thesis. Clearly I hadn't a clue what it was going on about and I spent most of the following autumn term trying to decipher it. Nick and his mate treated me with a kind of amused suspicion and with good cause - I really was shit. I remember after one mathematical discussion Nick shaking his head at me and saying, 'Sometimes I worry about you Chris.'

The pair of them lived in a run-down flat on Upper Parliament Street and often told me rat-related stories about it. Thankfully it was burnt down during the Toxteth riots – a night of rioting that I managed to sleep through in my flat at Philharmonic Court less than a hundred yards from the action.

Nick and his mates also took me to the Wolves v Arsenal FA Cup semi-final at Villa Park in 1979. Nick was arrested for, at least as far as I was concerned, understandably telling a copper not to shove him – the words, 'Get off me you fucking Pig', were hardly out of his mouth before he disappeared under a swarm of baton-wielding policemen. We all went down to support him at Wolverhampton Magistrates Court on the following Monday where he was unjustly fined £400 – a lot of money in those days.

I was outraged at the unfairness of it all but what can you do? Even today I think of Nick when I see a Wolves score.

Back to Hilary. In fact we were already courting, although my previous experience with women had taught me not to take anything for granted. It's all a bit hazy now, but I think my near year-long and dogged pursuit of her tall, long-haired loveliness began to pay dividends after she had finished her second year exams. All I can really remember for sure was inviting her to visit a funfair with me on one wonderfully warm summer's evening.

The fair was down in Sefton Park and we strolled down there from Morton: me eager and slightly disbelieving we were going on a kind of date and Hilary sceptical and amused by my behaviour. When we arrived at the entertainments I made the big mistake of taking her on a waltzer. It was a scenario I should have anticipated but trying to make Hilary like me must have been too distracting. We took our seats in a kind of giant teacup that can spin on its own central axis while simultaneously circulating on a roundabout. Even without any spinning I would have struggled to keep any food down and I was doing my best to appear relaxed and nonchalant, praying that I will be able to survive.

Of course, almost as soon as the ride began, one of the fairground workers (they must be trained to spot weakness) arrived and stood next to the waltzer grinning at us knowingly. That would have been irritating enough but he then began spinning us around despite my increasingly hysterical pleas to stop.

After the ride I had to stagger behind a caravan and throw up while Hilary looked away. Again the details are hazy but apart from that I must have made a favourable impression because I persuaded her to let me see her over the summer. I spent a number of weekends visiting her in Norfolk and meeting her family. I was besotted and it was a happy few months delving into her character and having days out in the beautiful city of Norwich and most of the beauty spots around North Walsham where she lived.

For six weeks of the summer I also went on a course at the Royal Greenwich Observatory down at Herstmonceux Castle in Sussex where I worked for Tony Sinclair, one of Jim Message's previous doctoral students. Even though my computing skills weren't much better than my mum's I got to work on an orbital programme for some Nasa space flight. Sorry, I've no idea which one or how the fuck I did it.

The castle was incredible and the civil servants who used to work there back then must have loved it. The food and my accommodation was great and I even got to observe Saturn one night through one of the telescopes. It looked so lonely out there in space and gave me the willies.

Every weekend was free and I either spent it at home in Devon or up in Norfolk with Hilary. The Cortina came into its own and the route up through Sussex and Kent, across the Thames and up to North Walsham via the A12, A140 are still etched in my memory.

It was on a journey back from Devon, however, that I had my first of many experiences of breaking down in the Cortina. People wonder why men of my age were so good at fixing cars when the answer is obvious – we had to be! That Monday I left Devon at 6.30 am and never made it to the castle until the evening. It pissed down with rain and at some god-forsaken place in Dorset, the car shuddered to a halt in the middle of nowhere. The AA sent out a mechanic who told me that water must have got into my petrol tank. He took me back to his garage and drained the tank and after a few hours I was on my way before breaking down again sometime later. The next day Tony and his boss decided to believe my far-fetched story and that was that. A year or so later I could have fixed the car myself after telling the mechanic to shove his ridiculous conclusions up his arse.

The summer came to an end. I was happy and hopelessly in love. Hilary, the object of my affections, was to spend the next year in Clermont

Ferrand as part of her French studies while I was to share a flat in Liverpool with Dave Peru and Mark Thompson.

9: Autumn Term 1978 – Spring 1979

The flat was on the second floor of a house of faded grandeur in Linnet Lane at the end away from Lark Lane, now a trendy enclave near Sefton Park and Aigburth Road. It was closer to town than Carnatic so I could walk into university and we had a happy year there. It also marked a departure from my usual safety-first approach to accommodation.

Mark, Dave and I knew fuck-all about living independently and consequently we made things up as we went along. I remember that none of us ever cooked in the horrible kitchen and lived quite independently in our own rooms. There were four bedrooms that led onto a wide, rectangular hallway that was topped by an ornate domed glass roof. During the winter the whole flat was amusingly cold – for example, one morning during a cold snap I discovered the toilet had frozen over (probably because the window in the bathroom was broken) when I went to have my first piss of the day.

Bob came and stayed in the fourth and spare room for a few weeks because at that stage of his medical studies his holidays didn't coincide with the usual academic year. For the rest of the time the three of us existed as best we could. None of us ever cooked a meal in the kitchen or had a bath in the bathroom because they were just too horrible to contemplate. I, for example, ate mostly at the student union building and washed in a bowl of hot water in my bedroom. In the winter it was freezing cold - there was no central heating and I remember sleeping in a track suit under a lot of blankets and a sleeping bag and it still only being just bearable.

Mark was into his hi fi system and lined the windows of his room with the polystyrene from the packaging from some new amplifier and turntable purchases. Dave usually wore at least three layers of clothing when he was up and about in his room getting some work done. One of our male-bonding pastimes was playing football with several socks rolled up into a ball – we'd stand in our own doorways trying to score through the doorway of our flatmates – childish but happy days.

By now I was well and truly involved with Wavertree Community Church. Hilary had taken me along to a few meetings before she went home in the Summer and I'd been introduced to the people there. Unfortunately this meant I didn't spend a lot of time with Dave or Mark which now is a source of regret. I'd become a full paid up member of the 'God Squad' which has a habit of making one, quite justifiably, a bit of a social pariah.

Anyway, my social life that year – if you can call it that - revolved around the church. I became friends with Alan and Les Kennedy who, years later, took over the Rose Hill C of E parish, Phil Metcalf and many others. Phil, a perpetually cheerful primary school teacher and famously single, was my mentor during this time and I spent a lot of time in his company.

I was entranced by the whole thing – I'd never been in church services where the worship was heart-felt and people spoke in tongues and prophesied. In fact I'd never been in a church service before – period, but I was pretty sure that your run of the mill Anglican or Catholic church didn't experience the stuff that I witnessed and was a part of. Being at Wavertree Community Church also gave me access to ordinary Liverpudlians for the first time. It all felt new and exciting and cutting edge.

Looking back they were all good people, led astray by the fairy tale of a real and ever-present God. I swallowed it hook, line and sinker as well and, in good old Chris Grayling style, was as fervent as anyone. Except that I was educated and also relatively normal and not averse to asking difficult questions. I'm not going to pretend that I wasn't completely committed to the cause, however, because I was. Plus I had Hilary as a kind of anchor to lean on when I wasn't sure about anything or anyone. She was a beacon of what I felt to be reasoned sanity in the perplexing new world that I found myself in. Apart from that I gladly put aside all my worldly experience, sacrificing it on the altar of belief in Jesus.

Hilary was away in France for the year I was in Linnet Lane and we wrote to each other every week. In fact all I did that year was letter writing or doing stuff associated with my studies or the church. I neglected my previous friendships because of this which is now a source of regret. I found Jesus and lost almost everything else.

The only thing of note that I can remember from that year was all tied up with the other new constant in my life – the Cortina. At some point I made friends with a guy called John who part owned a garage at the back of Linnet Lane where they rebuilt engines and otherwise improved the performance of cars like mine. God knows how it happened but at some point I needed a new engine and John provided one.

In order to save money I must have also put the car in the drive of the flat and not used it for a few months. The reason I remember this is because Dave and Mark helped me get it going for the first time after its lay-off. When I was ready to put it back on the road we push-started it down Linnet Lane. For some reason, I'd taken out the seats, so that when the car had reached a suitable speed and I jumped into it, it was all I could do to see where I was going by peering over the dashboard. It must have looked funny because Mark nearly swallowed the fag he was smoking at the time through laughing so much.

10: Summer 1979 to Autumn 1981: Student and Teacher

Those years are now only a blur so it seems only right that I intend to cover both in a single chapter. At their beginning I was still a postgraduate student and living with Dave and Mark. In May 1979 Margaret Thatcher came to power and, somewhere in America, the personal computer was invented. But I was largely ignorant of such momentous world events even though, to my embarrassment now, I remember actually voting for the Iron Lady. Dave was, quite rightly, disgusted.

Young people are mostly too self-obsessed to be concerned about the big things and I was no different. All I was foolishly convinced of was the validity of my faith in Christ and the innocent certainty that I was on the winning team in that regard. Since then, I've changed my mind, and the world seems a much more random place in which events are determined by man and nature.

Right now, in March 2022, the UK is apparently coming to the end of the pandemic. It feels like we are all bored by lockdowns rather than convinced by persuasive data. Many have yet to fully face up to the reality of climate change and the world-changing events that it will provoke. Even Putin, apparently untouchable in Russia, will, I think, learn the hard way that the world has changed –

people want freedom and money more than they want their countries to be all-conquering. Back then, however, in the late seventies and early eighties there were no obvious clouds on my or humanity's horizons.

Hilary's return from France was obviously the most anticipated event of the summer of 1979 as far as I was concerned. We saw a lot of each other after that which, I imagine, involved a lot of visits to North Walsham where her parents lived. She continued to show me around North Norfolk and Norwich and we were blissfully happy. I guess that these were the first summers when I didn't work at Radfords and so gradually lost contact with Terry and Janet. They are both dead now but I did squeeze in one last visit to see him in 2017. They were both in good form living in a redeveloped Radfords. Nothing ever stays the same and to be aware of the transient nature of things is to really grow up.

I must have taken Hilary down to Devon to meet my mum who was outwardly polite and welcoming. I wasn't her son for nothing, however, and knew that she still secretly harboured a loyalty towards the beautiful Teeny. She also wasn't keen on my new found faith either but she loved me enough to forgive my folly in that regard and to also grudgingly accept Hilary.

There was also a certain latent jealousy harboured by Hilary towards my mum. She sometimes complained that we visited her too much but I ignored her because she was wrong: I loved them both and my brother Steve apart, I was all my mum had. As the years went by it is worth noting that Hilary gradually won my mum around with her thoughtful and kind behaviour.

At some point I moved into a university flat in Philharmonic Court on Hope Street and Hilary got a room in the same complex. Seeing each other was, therefore, easy. She was back for her final year studying French which she seemed to take in her stride. Our social lives were dominated by the church where her elder sister Lorraine and her new husband Malcolm were, coincidently, members. Malcolm taught in Liverpool and Lorraine moved up to the city with him. She was very practically minded and, I thought, seemed a little surprised at the spiritual goings-on at the services, while Malcolm was a deacon and regularly spoke publicly in tongues.

Rather incongruously, Hilary seemed to me to be more spiritual than either of them as well as, for that matter, most of the other members of the church. I regarded her with the utmost spiritual respect as well as the usual emotions one associates with one's girlfriend. However, I was new to this Christianity thing and always felt that I was being indulged by the others, even her.

It seemed natural and inevitable that we would be married and so we were at Long Lane Methodist Church on June 28th, 1980. The wedding was in Liverpool rather than Norfolk because we both felt that Liverpool and, more specifically, Wavertree Community Church, was now our home rather than where Hilary had grown up. It was, of course, miles for my mum, Steve and Rog to come and now I regret the self-obsession that marked the occasion. Not unlike many couples we'd fallen into the trap of believing that we and our relationship was special when it wasn't. My best man was Alan Kennedy who, together with his wife Les, had befriended us since Hilary's return from France. Alan was a good guy but we had as much in common as a cat and a canary and now I wish I'd given Steve or Rog the nod. Everyone else from my pre-university past was absent which probably goes to show how I'd become totally immersed in the church and my faith.

After the service and reception meal we headed off in the car to Scotland. I drove like a maniac and we reached a B and B somewhere in the heart of the highlands for the first night. The next day we caught a ferry over to Skye where we honeymooned for a week in a crofter's cottage. It was like stepping back fifty years - I still remember vividly having a welcoming cup of tea in the farmer's mud-floored parlour and looking amusingly surprised as a chicken ran across the open doorway and into another room. Down south cats, dogs or even budgies were regarded as pet material rather than farm animals. Carpet or lino were also more prevalent than hardened mud.

The croft we had rented smelt and felt as damp as one of the local bogs but I was as happy as I'd ever been and was completely smitten by Hilary. We had a marvellous week looking around the island and even had a walk on the week's single sunny day.

Back in Liverpool, Hilary moved into the flat with me and we both signed up for teacher training at the Department of Education at the University. We were both serious about teaching but I also needed another year to work on the Ph D which was progressing at glacial speed. I spread my time between the education department, my office in the maths building and the church. Where teaching was concerned I figured I would be good at it. The long holidays were also appealing in so far as I like not working. I was also intelligent enough to see that being home when any children we might have were also off, was an obvious plus.

In early 1981 we did our teacher training, the memory of which provoked the writing of this book. I was lucky to get Blackburne House because it was a two minute walk away. All I can really remember is the old-fashioned staffroom with its piles of books and Mr Everett - except for one day when it snowed. It was freezing so I decided that I would wear my long-johns to keep warm. This was a mistake of epic proportions because all of my teaching that day was in a room where a radiator was positioned under the blackboard. In every lesson I was sweating like a pig in no time and soon had my pupils grinning at my discomfort. If they'd also known about my poor choice of underwear there would have been even more hilarity.

In the summer of 1981 I got a job at Wirral Grammar School for Girls in Bebington where I spent four happy years. When I started teaching it is interesting to note that smacking pupils wasn't against the law (although we never did it at WGS). I also saw the introduction of calculators into teaching and the consequent demise of log tables. Teacher-training or 'Baker Days' as they were known then, were introduced, and of course I used real chalk to write on the blackboards and became adept at getting into school early so I could use the Banda machine for copying worksheets rather than a photocopier as I did in later years.

I threw myself into the life of the school and appeared in all the staff productions where I was in demand as one of the few young men on the staff. In one of them I must have been playing a woman because I remember vividly the Mersey tunnel attendant giving my make-up and wig a suspicious once-over one night when I was driving back home.

I also fell over in a Year Seven lesson which caused a collective melt-down. In my defence the floor was highly polished and my shoes also had slippery soles. Even I laughed while noting never to make abrupt changes of direction in a lesson again.

As is my wont I also regaled the girls with any interesting incidents from my own life including the time an old lady ran into the side of my car just before I was coming onto the ramp up to the Mersey tunnel. I'd seen her up ahead trying to run across the road, and by accelerating I'd probably saved her life by avoiding running her over. I remember Lorna Wakefield laughing uncontrollably as I pointed out how surprised the lady had looked even as her nose squashed into the window of the passenger door. Or course I stopped when, in the rear view mirror, I saw that, as a result of the collision, the woman was engaged in a spiralling descent onto the dual carriageway. She turned out to be fine although Lorna nearly died from laughing so much.

On another occasion one little shit of a Year Nine stood up to me in a class and called me a 'Big-headed sod'. In later years I would have laughed and dealt with it myself but back then the deputy head had to be called. Downstairs in her office she gave the girl a bollocking and a suitable punishment. In the staffroom afterwards we had a laugh about it, everyone agreeing that I actually was a big-headed sod.

At Wirral I learnt my trade teaching maths. I enjoyed the staffroom and especially the company of David Nadin who taught economics and Barry Thomas who came over from the boys' high school after our mad Head of Art resigned. She'd been known to dance naked in the quadrangle, something I'm glad to report, that I never witnessed. Barry was full of hilarious stories about teaching in the old days including one where an old Head of Year Eleven at his school had caned a boy on a pedestrian crossing in Bebington High Street. According to Barry all of the onlookers clapped once the teacher had finished. In case you're wondering the boy in question had chucked a brick through the staffroom window and the teacher had had to chase him into Bebington.

My HOD was a guy called Harry Markham from, believe it or not, Devon. He was old school in so far as he could teach brilliantly but never did any discernible work. Consequently he left me alone which was just fine by me. There are other staff I remember of course and a few random girls like Katy Raftery, Lorna Wakefield and the aptly named Janet Greatbanks. Katy's two claims to fame were being sufficiently pleasant not to eliminate us christening our firstborn Katie and also for shouting out 'give her one Mr Grayling' during a staff production when my character was locked in an embrace with some blonde teacher whom I can no longer remember.

I drove over from Liverpool every day until the Cortina died, soon to be followed by an old Mark 2 that I picked up for £25 from an incredulous dealer on Green Lane not far from Stoneville Road in the Old Swan district where we lived. After the engine in that one expired in a puff of smoke in Birkenhead on the way to school I caught the bus, the underground under the Mersey and another bus to get to work. The journey took over an hour but I took it in my stride – one of the benefits of youth.

Sometime during those four years I finally got the Ph. D. even if my viva with Jim Message and Tony Sinclair was one of the most embarrassing experiences of my life! In retrospect I should have checked what a spherical pendulum was. Still, I was now a doctor and I regarded my university education as finally over.

11: Autumn 1981 to Summer 1985: Married and Teaching

Hilary and I lived with her sister Loraine and Malcolm when we first started teaching. Hilary also worked on the Wirral at a girls' secondary modern and we spent six happy weeks living in their front room before moving into our own terraced house in Stoneville Road. Hilary's Head of Department was loaded and I remember eating caviar at her house on the only staff do we attended there.

25 Stoneville Road, our first house, cost us £16,500 in 1981 and was a three bedroomed terraced house with generously proportioned rooms. Several Wavertree Church members lived either in the street or just around the corner but our neighbours Jean and Alistair were the best. Jean was unfailingly pleasant and Alistair helped me out of many holes on both the car and house front. He even took me over to the Wirral to work on a couple of occasions when the Cortina wouldn't start.

On the other side of Alistair and Jean lived another couple and two lovely children. We didn't have much to do with them except for once when I had a vivid dream about the mother. I woke up convinced that I was married to her until, with relief, I saw Hilary's head on the pillow next to me.

While we lived there I rekindled my badminton playing and joined a club over near Rock

Ferry station on the Wirral. I used to catch the train over there but that's about all I remember except for a couple of blokes who played there. One of them was called Brian, who I knew from the university club and the other was Rikki Brown who, I think, owed a sports shop in the area. The former was also a teacher at a comp and described an interesting experiment he'd conducted with his students. For one year he set a weekly homework and, during the next, given the class nothing. He found his GCSE results were unchanged by these two different approaches.

Rikki's influence was much more personal. Around that time I'd noticed one day that a bald patch was beginning to appear on the top of my head. He claimed that he had the answer to my distress. During some off court chit-chat he said that he was taking a daily dose of cyder vinegar and black molasses which seemed to be reversing his own baldness. I was dubious but desperate and went home and tried it for myself. As I'm now bald I think we can safely say that Rikki's remedy failed. It also tasted horrible.

The only other things of note I recall from those times were running, Mozart and a TV-less house. The first was fun and I ran the Wirral half marathon with Bob Edwards who left me in his wake with about five miles to go. Believe it or not I ran the whole way in a track suit so I must have been fitter than I am now when even breaking into a jog is considered pushing at my physical boundaries. My other running adventures were a couple of 10K races, both also on the Wirral and the Liverpool half marathon. Norman, my best friend from the church, and another guy from church called John entered one of the 10Ks with me. In those days Norman was a bit of a couch potato and just made it around. He gave the Liverpool half marathon a miss, however, but John and I trained for it, if you'll forgive the expression, religiously. I made it around in about one and a half hours and that, my friends, is the last time I ran in a race.

For some unknown reason I also became interested in classical music around then. Perhaps I'd started a collection with some cut-price records from a club? Anyway, it wasn't long before I'd fallen in love with Mozart and his music and used every opportunity to listen to it. Ginny's father, a classical music fan who often took Ginny and I to concerts at the Liverpool Philharmonic, would have been impressed. I even went to the trouble to record Mozart concerts off the radio.

Incredibly, Hilary and I spent most of our four years in Stoneville without a TV except for an old black and white one that I bought from some second hand shop during our final year in Liverpool. It was really only so that I could watch Steve Ovett races and other athletic shows but that was about the extent of my viewing. It's probably also worth mentioning at this point that Hilary's parents also owned a black and white TV. They could have had a colour one like the rest of the country but were just too tight to contemplate the extra expense. They also knocked the giving of Christmas presents between adults on the head although one year they did splash out on a single white handkerchief for me. 'You shouldn't have,' I spluttered, never meaning three words more sincerely.

At some point in 1982 Hilary's irritation with her own mother erupted into a row between them and us. They didn't speak to us for over a year until Katie was born and we invited them up to meet her. Their silence didn't bother me much (it meant less driving to their new house in Suffolk) but I was surprised at Hilary's mum that she didn't make some overtures at some point before we held out the olive branch. I suppose that'll teach me to expect Christian behaviour from Christians.

We lived in Stoneville Road until we moved down to Tunbridge Wells via Woodbridge to where Hilary's parents had moved. Despite my gradually advancing disenchantment with the church they were happy days. Hilary and I were in love and we enjoyed the other's company. We made some good friends, chiefly Norman and Chris who lived in a flat around the corner in Kremlin Drive until they bought a house in Stoneville. Unfortunately, among other things, church politics came between us soon after. Thankfully, I'm friends again with Norm even though he lives in New Zealand and we both have different wives.

We spent a lot of time around at their flat and were spiritually very close even though I only discovered recently that Chris was a woman who had undergone a lot of previous traumas. Norm was a great guitarist and song writer and even wrote a song about our relationship. The gravity of it all is now lost in the sands of time but the first time he sang it one Sunday evening during a church service was a truly powerful and moving experience.

They came around for dinner a few times and on one such occasion we had a laugh. Hilary produced a chocolate cream cake for pudding which I thought tasted funny. I pulled it apart to reveal a healthy colony of bacteria attacking the filling. 'Stop - ,' I shouted to Norman in vain. It was too late – he'd already swallowed a huge mouthful.

Working on the Cortina was a kind of obsession while we were at Stoneville. I even changed the back axle after picking one up on one of my many trips to the scrapyards down on the Dock Road. I'd made friends with Mark from Church - a guy who worked at the local abattoir and smelt much like a decaying horse carcass himself. Still, he brought me around some brake fluid when I couldn't get the brakes to work after the transplant and in the end we got them functioning. We went inside for a celebratory cuppa after which, as was usual practice, Hilary had to wash the chair he'd sat in to remove the smell he always left.

We were burgled once while we lived there and some lads tried to nick the car a couple of times. I'd disconnected the distributor cap so they were unsuccessful and on one occasion my neighbours were treated to the sight of me running up the road in my pyjamas after them as they tried to push start the car.

Katie was born in January 1984 and was toddling about by the time we left in July 1985. Hilary was a couple of weeks overdue before she was born so we went to a James Bond film in the city centre hoping that the excitement would get things moving. It did and the next day my beautiful eldest daughter was born at Edge Lane Maternity Hospital.

In the following months we paraded her proudly in her pram around Old Swan on Saturday mornings and to all our friends. I remember Ray Brown, a great guy who lived around the corner and worked at the old Cammell Laird shipyard, remarking affectionately on the size of her nose as she slept in her pram. I also nearly knocked myself out while she was having a bath by hitting my forehead on the room's doorframe as I was jumping into the room trying to surprise her.

Hilary wasn't keen but she went back to work in order to keep her maternity pay. Katie was child-minded by Pete and Heather Pretlove from the church. They were southerners like us and had both trained as primary school teachers.

I loved Liverpool but realised that I needed to move on if I was to have any kind of career. The grammar schools of Kent seemed like the most obvious option. I'd never wanted to teach in the private sector so it never crossed my mind to apply there.

Miss Baines and the other staff at Wirral were lovely to me but I was excited by the prospect of moving south to Kent. In her speech to the school on my leaving day I remember her saluting my professionalism. Half an hour later I was with the other teachers in the staff room having a drink when I was called to one of its doors to say goodbye to some students. A tall, dark and attractive sixth-former kissed me on the lips and I remember a teacher passing us and remarking wryly 'very professional'.

And that's about it – a week or so later I drove a hired Luton van containing our furniture down to Woodbridge to join Hilary and Katie and the newly born Sophie Alice. I was still in Liverpool when she was born so I'd missed her birth in

Ipswich. Hilary had wisely thought it would be easier without me getting in the way.

April 2022

So, here I am nearly thirty-seven years later. I left Liverpool when I was thirty so I hope that puts things in perspective. After Sophie was born in the August of 1985 it wasn't until March 1989 that Lucie, my third and last daughter was born. They have all been a delight although, to be fair, Hilary and I were great parents.

Unfortunately, however, I turned out to be terrible husband material and Hilary sensibly divorced me before the new millennium kicked off. Since then, believe it or not, I found Theresa Dickens who turned out to be the love of my life. It just goes to show that men need to be at least forty before they can be allowed to make reliable decisions about love.

I taught at TWGGS for twenty two years and had a lot of fun before falling out with the Head in 2007. Since then I've had a whale of a time tutoring, writing and renovating a house with Mrs Dickens. Despite the ravages of old age, I'm happier now than I ever was in Liverpool or Devon but I remember those times and the people who enhanced my life back then with great fondness. Quite undeservingly, I've been a lucky bastard and I thank my lucky stars.

A Few Photos

Teeny

With Rog and Cindy at Bill's Wedding

Hilary and Katie

Me and Rog get our shirts off.

Dave Peru

I take the Cortina to Liverpool for the first time

Janet and Terry Crump

Printed in Great Britain
by Amazon